STAI__ _____

GRATITUDE

A 26 Week
Gratitude Journal

Change your habits, change your life!

Marc Reklau

Start with Gratitude © 2019 by Marc Reklau
All rights reserved.
Cover design: galuhh
Printed by Amazon

Disclaimer

This book is designed to provide information and motivation to our readers. It is sold with the understanding that the publisher is not engaged to render any type of psychological, legal, or any other kind of professional advice. The instructions and advice in this book are not intended as a substitute for counseling. The content of each chapter is the sole expression and opinion of its author. No warranties or guarantees are expressed or implied by the author's and publisher's choice to include any of the content in this volume. Neither the publisher nor the individual author shall be liable for any physical, psychological, emotional, financial, or commercial damages, including, but not limited to, special, incidental, consequential or other damages. Our views and rights are the same:

You must test everything for yourself according to your own situation talents and aspirations

You are responsible for your own decisions, choices, actions, and results.

Marc Reklau

Visit my website at www.marcreklau.com

ISBN-13:: 9781703267785
Imprint: Independently published

This
Gratitude Journal

belongs to

It all starts with gratitude

I've you have heard me speak or read some of my books, you know that I'm a huge fan of gratitude. As a matter of fact, I consider it one of the most important ingredients to my success. The more grateful I was, the more successful I became.

One of my top "tools" was a simple gratitude journal, which I used to answer a couple of simple questions every day. My book "The Life-changing Power of Gratitude" already includes a 90-Day Gratitude journal, so the logical next step was to put out an entire 26 weeks gratitude journal. Half a year of gratitude will almost probably have an enormous impact on your life.

It's simple. Answer the 5 questions every day. **Feel the gratitude and the joy while you are doing it** (This is crucial) and look what happens. Probably miracles. But don't take my word for it. Take the results of countless studies about the subject. .

Practicing gratitude regularly will do the following for you:
Gratitude is one of the most powerful forces in the universe, and being grateful not only brings good things into our lives but also makes us notice more and more of those things that are already there. And when I talk about practicing gratitude, I don't talk about practicing it once a year or every now and then. I talk about practicing it every single day and throughout each day. Make gratitude a lifestyle.

If you want to know more, you might enjoy my book "The Life-changing Power of Gratitude," where I explain everything I found out about gratitude and give you seven simple exercises that will change your life. Or you can just get to work with this journal. I'm sure it will do its work for you, and you will enjoy the countless benefits of gratitude.

When you appreciate things, they grow. Appreciate every breath, appreciate every flower, enjoy your friends' company more. When you appreciate the good in your life, the good grows.

Gratitude is really the best antidote to all the negative emotions. Why? Because you can't feel any kind of worry, anger, or depression while you practice gratitude. You can't even get upset about your current life circumstances while you're practicing gratitude. You can't be grateful and unhappy at the same time. You can't be grateful and worried at the same time. It's just not possible.

In a study conducted by Robert Emmons and Michael McCullough from UC Davis, people who wrote down five things they were grateful for every night before going to bed were more optimistic, happier, healthier, more generous, more benevolent, and much more likely to achieve their goals than people who didn't write anything down, wrote down five hassles, or wrote down five things they were better at than others.

Gratitude recharges you with energy, boosts your self-worth, and is directly linked to physical and mental well-being. It leads you directly to happiness, and as I mentioned before, it's the best antidote to anger, envy, and resentment.

Gratitude improves not only your health and mindset but also your relationships (which, by the way, are the number one predictor of your future happiness and success). If you spend time being grateful every day, you will naturally become happier.

Further proven benefits of the "Attitude of Gratitude" are increased confidence, improved health, fewer headaches, better sleep, and an increased level of enjoying life experiences. Another positive side effect is that as you become happier, you naturally "attract" people, things, and situations that make you happier and, thus, create a life that is beyond your wildest imagination. That's the power of gratitude, the most powerful force in the universe.

Researchers found that doing the gratitude exercises for just one week will make you happier and less depressed, and you'll see a significant difference after one, three, and six months. You'll even remain significantly happier and show higher levels of optimism after stopping the exercises. Still, I highly recommend you keep on doing the exercises because they will do miracles for you. You'll get better and better at scanning the world for good things and writing them down. You'll see more and more opportunities wherever you look without even trying.

Why Journaling

Writing everything down in your journal will give you an extra boost of happiness, motivation, and self-esteem every morning and evening.

The great thing is that just before going to sleep, you will be focusing on positive things, which will have a beneficial effect on your sleep and your subconscious mind. Why? Because your focus will be on the positive things of the day and gratitude instead of the negative things and things that didn't work well, which would probably keep you awake.

Don't worry if the words don't start flowing right away when you do the exercise the first time. It's a matter of practice. If you are blocked and can't think of anything, just stay with it for five minutes longer. Trust that the answers will come. Write the first things that come to mind without overthinking them or judging them. These things are often correct.

Don't worry about your style or mistakes. Just write! Do this every day for a month, and observe the changes that take place! A regular notebook or calendar will do.

Studies found out that journaling improves your focus, lowers stress, and has countless other health benefits.

A study by the Department of Psychological Medicine, University of Auckland, New Zealand, from 2013 even found that journaling promotes faster wound healing! The members of the journaling group healed over 75% faster than their non-journaling counterparts.

Further research shows that journaling results in reduced absenteeism from work, quicker reemployment after a job loss, and higher GPAs for students. Think about it. People who wrote in their journal for as little as fifteen minutes a day healed their wounds faster, improved their immune systems, and improved their GPAs.

I'm always insisting so much on writing things down, and people ask me why they can't just practice gratitude in their minds.

The answer is: Because writing about things puts them in perspective. By writing things down, you structure and organize your thoughts and feelings. As a result, you will sleep, feel, and think better. You'll even have a more vibrant social life. Almost certainly, your journaling will create momentum because you are reinforcing the positive over and over again.

Another advantage of journaling is that you start to understand things better—most of all, yourself. You can find success patterns and discover how you can grow and learn from situations, which situations to avoid, how to react better, how to succeed faster next time, and which opportunities to seize. You will simply allow yourself to take inventory of all the positive moments of your day—the big ones and the small ones. Doing this every night, you will build massive levels of confidence. Taking your life to the next level will become inevitable.

Make them a habit. Ritualize them. Do them at the same time each day. Keep what you need to do these exercises readily available and convenient.

For example, keep a journal on your nightstand. Clients of mine have told me that they had a lot of fun and got great results doing the exercises with children and spouses.

Don't give up if things don't go smoothly at first. It needs some time, but slowly, you'll get better and better at it thanks to the magic of discipline and repetition.

You should have five minutes a day to do these exercises no matter what your situation is. Tony Robbins once said, "If you don't have five minutes a day, you don't have a life."

Make gratitude a daily habit. When you are grateful for what you have, more things that you can be grateful for will come into your life. So be grateful for what you have and even for the things you don't have yet.

Stop comparing. Practice gratitude instead. Count your blessings instead of other people's blessings. This exercise alone can probably "cure" you of jealousy and envy if you practice it for three to four weeks.

Gratitude is not a magic pill, although it certainly has all the ingredients. Once you do the work in the real world, magic happens. I wish you this magic. All the best!

Marc

Week 1

As we express our gratitude, we must never forget that the highest appreciation is not to utter words, but to live by them.   John F. Kennedy

Date:_____/_____/_____

Three things I'm grateful for:

_____
_____
_____
_____

Three things that I did particularly well today:

_____
_____
_____
_____

Three positive things that happened today:

_____
_____
_____
_____

How could I have made today even better?

_____
_____
_____
_____

What is my most important goal for tomorrow?

_____
_____
_____
_____

Date:_____/_____/_____

Three things I'm grateful for:

_____
_____
_____
_____

Three things that I did particularly well today:

_____
_____
_____
_____

Three positive things that happened today:

_____
_____
_____
_____

How could I have made today even better?

_____
_____
_____
_____

What is my most important goal for tomorrow?

_____
_____
_____
_____

Date:_____/_____/_____

Three things I'm grateful for:

_____

_____

_____

_____

Three things that I did particularly well today:

_____

_____

_____

_____

Three positive things that happened today:

_____

_____

_____

_____

How could I have made today even better?

_____

_____

_____

_____

What is my most important goal for tomorrow?

_____

_____

_____

_____

Date:_____/_____/_____

Three things I'm grateful for:

_____
_____
_____
_____

Three things that I did particularly well today:

_____
_____
_____
_____

Three positive things that happened today:

_____
_____
_____
_____

How could I have made today even better?

_____
_____
_____
_____

What is my most important goal for tomorrow?

_____
_____
_____
_____

Date:_____/_____/_____

Three things I'm grateful for:

_____
_____
_____
_____

Three things that I did particularly well today:

_____
_____
_____
_____

Three positive things that happened today:

_____
_____
_____
_____

How could I have made today even better?

_____
_____
_____
_____

What is my most important goal for tomorrow?

_____
_____
_____
_____

Date:_____/_____/_____

Three things I'm grateful for:

_____

_____

_____

_____

Three things that I did particularly well today:

_____

_____

_____

_____

Three positive things that happened today:

_____

_____

_____

_____

How could I have made today even better?

_____

_____

_____

_____

What is my most important goal for tomorrow?

_____

_____

_____

_____

Date:_____/_____/_____

Three things I'm grateful for:

_____

_____

_____

_____

Three things that I did particularly well today:

_____

_____

_____

_____

Three positive things that happened today:

_____

_____

_____

_____

How could I have made today even better?

_____

_____

_____

_____

What is my most important goal for tomorrow?

_____

_____

_____

_____

Week 2

Gratitude makes sense of our past, brings peace for today, and creates a vision for tomorrow.

Melody Beattie

Date:_____/_____/_____

Three things I'm grateful for:

_____
_____
_____
_____

Three things that I did particularly well today:

_____
_____
_____
_____

Three positive things that happened today:

_____
_____
_____
_____

How could I have made today even better?

_____
_____
_____
_____

What is my most important goal for tomorrow?

_____
_____
_____
_____

Date:_____/_____/_____

Three things I'm grateful for:

_____
_____
_____
_____

Three things that I did particularly well today:

_____
_____
_____
_____

Three positive things that happened today:

_____
_____
_____
_____

How could I have made today even better?

_____
_____
_____
_____

What is my most important goal for tomorrow?

_____
_____
_____
_____

Date:_____/_____/_____

Three things I'm grateful for:

_____
_____
_____
_____

Three things that I did particularly well today:

_____
_____
_____
_____

Three positive things that happened today:

_____
_____
_____
_____

How could I have made today even better?

_____
_____
_____
_____

What is my most important goal for tomorrow?

_____
_____
_____
_____

Date:_____/_____/_____

Three things I'm grateful for:

_____
_____
_____
_____

Three things that I did particularly well today:

_____
_____
_____
_____

Three positive things that happened today:

_____
_____
_____
_____

How could I have made today even better?

_____
_____
_____
_____

What is my most important goal for tomorrow?

_____
_____
_____
_____

Date:_____/_____/_____

Three things I'm grateful for:

_____
_____
_____
_____

Three things that I did particularly well today:

_____
_____
_____
_____

Three positive things that happened today:

_____
_____
_____
_____

How could I have made today even better?

_____
_____
_____
_____

What is my most important goal for tomorrow?

_____
_____
_____
_____

Date:_____/_____/_____

Three things I'm grateful for:

_____
_____
_____
_____

Three things that I did particularly well today:

_____
_____
_____
_____

Three positive things that happened today:

_____
_____
_____
_____

How could I have made today even better?

_____
_____
_____
_____

What is my most important goal for tomorrow?

_____
_____
_____
_____

Date:_____/_____/_____

Three things I'm grateful for:

_____

_____

_____

_____

Three things that I did particularly well today:

_____

_____

_____

_____

Three positive things that happened today:

_____

_____

_____

_____

How could I have made today even better?

_____

_____

_____

_____

What is my most important goal for tomorrow?

_____

_____

_____

_____

Week 3

Gratitude can transform common days into thanksgivings, turn routine jobs into joy, and change ordinary opportunities into blessings.

William Arthur Ward

Date:_____/_____/_____

Three things I'm grateful for:

_____

_____

_____

_____

Three things that I did particularly well today:

_____

_____

_____

_____

Three positive things that happened today:

_____

_____

_____

_____

How could I have made today even better?

_____

_____

_____

_____

What is my most important goal for tomorrow?

_____

_____

_____

_____

Date:_____ /_____ /_____

Three things I'm grateful for:

_____
_____
_____
_____

Three things that I did particularly well today:

_____
_____
_____
_____

Three positive things that happened today:

_____
_____
_____
_____

How could I have made today even better?

_____
_____
_____
_____

What is my most important goal for tomorrow?

_____
_____
_____
_____

Date:_____/_____/_____

Three things I'm grateful for:

_____
_____
_____
_____

Three things that I did particularly well today:

_____
_____
_____
_____

Three positive things that happened today:

_____
_____
_____
_____

How could I have made today even better?

_____
_____
_____
_____

What is my most important goal for tomorrow?

_____
_____
_____
_____

Date:_____/_____/_____

Three things I'm grateful for:

_____

_____

_____

_____

Three things that I did particularly well today:

_____

_____

_____

_____

Three positive things that happened today:

_____

_____

_____

_____

How could I have made today even better?

_____

_____

_____

_____

What is my most important goal for tomorrow?

_____

_____

_____

_____

Date:_____/_____/_____

Three things I'm grateful for:

_____
_____
_____
_____

Three things that I did particularly well today:

_____
_____
_____
_____

Three positive things that happened today:

_____
_____
_____
_____

How could I have made today even better?

_____
_____
_____
_____

What is my most important goal for tomorrow?

_____
_____
_____
_____

Date:_____/_____/_____

Three things I'm grateful for:

_____
_____
_____
_____

Three things that I did particularly well today:

_____
_____
_____
_____

Three positive things that happened today:

_____
_____
_____
_____

How could I have made today even better?

_____
_____
_____
_____

What is my most important goal for tomorrow?

_____
_____
_____
_____

Date:_____/_____/_____

Three things I'm grateful for:

_____
_____
_____
_____

Three things that I did particularly well today:

_____
_____
_____
_____

Three positive things that happened today:

_____
_____
_____
_____

How could I have made today even better?

_____
_____
_____
_____

What is my most important goal for tomorrow?

_____
_____
_____
_____

Week 4

'Thank you' is the best prayer that anyone could say. I say that one a lot. Thank you expresses extreme gratitude, humility, understanding.

Alice Walker

Date:_____/_____/_____

Three things I'm grateful for:

_____
_____
_____
_____

Three things that I did particularly well today:

_____
_____
_____
_____

Three positive things that happened today:

_____
_____
_____
_____

How could I have made today even better?

_____
_____
_____
_____

What is my most important goal for tomorrow?

_____
_____
_____
_____

Date:_____/_____/_____

Three things I'm grateful for:

_____

_____

_____

_____

Three things that I did particularly well today:

_____

_____

_____

_____

Three positive things that happened today:

_____

_____

_____

_____

How could I have made today even better?

_____

_____

_____

_____

What is my most important goal for tomorrow?

_____

_____

_____

_____

Date:_____/_____/_____

Three things I'm grateful for:

_____

_____

_____

_____

Three things that I did particularly well today:

_____

_____

_____

_____

Three positive things that happened today:

_____

_____

_____

_____

How could I have made today even better?

_____

_____

_____

_____

What is my most important goal for tomorrow?

_____

_____

_____

_____

Date:_____/_____/_____

Three things I'm grateful for:

Three things that I did particularly well today:

Three positive things that happened today:

How could I have made today even better?

What is my most important goal for tomorrow?

Date:_____/_____/_____

Three things I'm grateful for:

_____
_____
_____
_____

Three things that I did particularly well today:

_____
_____
_____
_____

Three positive things that happened today:

_____
_____
_____
_____

How could I have made today even better?

_____
_____
_____
_____

What is my most important goal for tomorrow?

_____
_____
_____
_____

Date:_____/_____/_____

Three things I'm grateful for:

_____
_____
_____
_____

Three things that I did particularly well today:

_____
_____
_____
_____

Three positive things that happened today:

_____
_____
_____
_____

How could I have made today even better?

_____
_____
_____
_____

What is my most important goal for tomorrow?

_____
_____
_____
_____

Date:_____/_____/_____

Three things I'm grateful for:

_____

_____

_____

_____

Three things that I did particularly well today:

_____

_____

_____

_____

Three positive things that happened today:

_____

_____

_____

_____

How could I have made today even better?

_____

_____

_____

_____

What is my most important goal for tomorrow?

_____

_____

_____

_____

Week 5

I am happy because I'm grateful. I choose to be grateful. That gratitude allows me to be happy.

Will Arnett

Date:_____/_____/_____

Three things I'm grateful for:

_____
_____
_____
_____

Three things that I did particularly well today:

_____
_____
_____
_____

Three positive things that happened today:

_____
_____
_____
_____

How could I have made today even better?

_____
_____
_____
_____

What is my most important goal for tomorrow?

_____
_____
_____
_____

Date:_____/_____/_____

Three things I'm grateful for:

_____

_____

_____

_____

Three things that I did particularly well today:

_____

_____

_____

_____

Three positive things that happened today:

_____

_____

_____

_____

How could I have made today even better?

_____

_____

_____

_____

What is my most important goal for tomorrow?

_____

_____

_____

_____

Date:_____/_____/_____

Three things I'm grateful for:

_____
_____
_____
_____

Three things that I did particularly well today:

_____
_____
_____
_____

Three positive things that happened today:

_____
_____
_____
_____

How could I have made today even better?

_____
_____
_____
_____

What is my most important goal for tomorrow?

_____
_____
_____
_____

Date:_____ / _____ / _____

Three things I'm grateful for:

Three things that I did particularly well today:

Three positive things that happened today:

How could I have made today even better?

What is my most important goal for tomorrow?

Date:_____/_____/_____

Three things I'm grateful for:

_____
_____
_____
_____

Three things that I did particularly well today:

_____
_____
_____
_____

Three positive things that happened today:

_____
_____
_____
_____

How could I have made today even better?

_____
_____
_____
_____

What is my most important goal for tomorrow?

_____
_____
_____
_____

Date:_____/_____/_____

Three things I'm grateful for:

_____
_____
_____
_____

Three things that I did particularly well today:

_____
_____
_____
_____

Three positive things that happened today:

_____
_____
_____
_____

How could I have made today even better?

_____
_____
_____
_____

What is my most important goal for tomorrow?

_____
_____
_____
_____

Date:_____/_____/_____

Three things I'm grateful for:

_____

_____

_____

_____

Three things that I did particularly well today:

_____

_____

_____

_____

Three positive things that happened today:

_____

_____

_____

_____

How could I have made today even better?

_____

_____

_____

_____

What is my most important goal for tomorrow?

_____

_____

_____

_____

Week 6

Gratitude is one of the strongest and most transformative states of being. It shifts your perspective from lack to abundance and allows you to focus on the good in your life, which in turn pulls more goodness into your reality.

Jen Sincero

Date:_____/_____/_____

Three things I'm grateful for:

_____
_____
_____
_____

Three things that I did particularly well today:

_____
_____
_____
_____

Three positive things that happened today:

_____
_____
_____
_____

How could I have made today even better?

_____
_____
_____
_____

What is my most important goal for tomorrow?

_____
_____
_____
_____

Date:_____/_____/_____

Three things I'm grateful for:

_____
_____
_____
_____

Three things that I did particularly well today:

_____
_____
_____
_____

Three positive things that happened today:

_____
_____
_____
_____

How could I have made today even better?

_____
_____
_____
_____

What is my most important goal for tomorrow?

_____
_____
_____
_____

Date:_____/_____/_____

Three things I'm grateful for:

_____
_____
_____
_____

Three things that I did particularly well today:

_____
_____
_____
_____

Three positive things that happened today:

_____
_____
_____
_____

How could I have made today even better?

_____
_____
_____
_____

What is my most important goal for tomorrow?

_____
_____
_____
_____

Date:_____/_____/_____

Three things I'm grateful for:

_____

_____

_____

_____

Three things that I did particularly well today:

_____

_____

_____

_____

Three positive things that happened today:

_____

_____

_____

_____

How could I have made today even better?

_____

_____

_____

_____

What is my most important goal for tomorrow?

_____

_____

_____

_____

Date:_____/_____/_____

Three things I'm grateful for:

_____
_____
_____
_____

Three things that I did particularly well today:

_____
_____
_____
_____

Three positive things that happened today:

_____
_____
_____
_____

How could I have made today even better?

_____
_____
_____
_____

What is my most important goal for tomorrow?

_____
_____
_____
_____

Date:_____/_____/_____

Three things I'm grateful for:

_____
_____
_____
_____

Three things that I did particularly well today:

_____
_____
_____
_____

Three positive things that happened today:

_____
_____
_____
_____

How could I have made today even better?

_____
_____
_____
_____

What is my most important goal for tomorrow?

_____
_____
_____
_____

Date:_____/_____/_____

Three things I'm grateful for:

_____

_____

_____

_____

Three things that I did particularly well today:

_____

_____

_____

_____

Three positive things that happened today:

_____

_____

_____

_____

How could I have made today even better?

_____

_____

_____

_____

What is my most important goal for tomorrow?

_____

_____

_____

_____

Week 7

Give yourself a gift of five minutes of contemplation in awe of everything you see around you. Go outside and turn your attention to the many miracles around you. This five-minute-a-day regimen of appreciation and gratitude will help you to focus your life in awe.

Wayne Dyer

Date:_____/_____/_____

Three things I'm grateful for:

_____

_____

_____

_____

Three things that I did particularly well today:

_____

_____

_____

_____

Three positive things that happened today:

_____

_____

_____

_____

How could I have made today even better?

_____

_____

_____

_____

What is my most important goal for tomorrow?

_____

_____

_____

_____

Date:_____/_____/_____

Three things I'm grateful for:

_____
_____
_____
_____

Three things that I did particularly well today:

_____
_____
_____
_____

Three positive things that happened today:

_____
_____
_____
_____

How could I have made today even better?

_____
_____
_____
_____

What is my most important goal for tomorrow?

_____
_____
_____
_____

Date:_____/_____/_____

Three things I'm grateful for:

_____
_____
_____
_____

Three things that I did particularly well today:

_____
_____
_____
_____

Three positive things that happened today:

_____
_____
_____
_____

How could I have made today even better?

_____
_____
_____
_____

What is my most important goal for tomorrow?

_____
_____
_____
_____

Date:_____/_____/_____

Three things I'm grateful for:

_____
_____
_____
_____

Three things that I did particularly well today:

_____
_____
_____
_____

Three positive things that happened today:

_____
_____
_____
_____

How could I have made today even better?

_____
_____
_____
_____

What is my most important goal for tomorrow?

_____
_____
_____
_____

Date:_____/_____/_____

Three things I'm grateful for:

_____

_____

_____

_____

Three things that I did particularly well today:

_____

_____

_____

_____

Three positive things that happened today:

_____

_____

_____

_____

How could I have made today even better?

_____

_____

_____

_____

What is my most important goal for tomorrow?

_____

_____

_____

_____

Date:_____/_____/_____

Three things I'm grateful for:

_____
_____
_____
_____

Three things that I did particularly well today:

_____
_____
_____
_____

Three positive things that happened today:

_____
_____
_____
_____

How could I have made today even better?

_____
_____
_____
_____

What is my most important goal for tomorrow?

_____
_____
_____
_____

Date:_____/_____/_____

Three things I'm grateful for:

_____
_____
_____
_____

Three things that I did particularly well today:

_____
_____
_____
_____

Three positive things that happened today:

_____
_____
_____
_____

How could I have made today even better?

_____
_____
_____
_____

What is my most important goal for tomorrow?

_____
_____
_____
_____

Week 8

I don't have to chase extraordinary moments to find happiness - it's right in front of me if I'm paying attention and practicing gratitude.

Brene Brown

Date:_____/_____/_____

Three things I'm grateful for:

_____

_____

_____

_____

Three things that I did particularly well today:

_____

_____

_____

_____

Three positive things that happened today:

_____

_____

_____

_____

How could I have made today even better?

_____

_____

_____

_____

What is my most important goal for tomorrow?

_____

_____

_____

_____

Date:_____ / _____ / _____

Three things I'm grateful for:

_____
_____
_____
_____

Three things that I did particularly well today:

_____
_____
_____
_____

Three positive things that happened today:

_____
_____
_____
_____

How could I have made today even better?

_____
_____
_____
_____

What is my most important goal for tomorrow?

_____
_____
_____
_____

Date:_____/_____/_____

Three things I'm grateful for:

_____
_____
_____
_____

Three things that I did particularly well today:

_____
_____
_____
_____

Three positive things that happened today:

_____
_____
_____
_____

How could I have made today even better?

_____
_____
_____
_____

What is my most important goal for tomorrow?

_____
_____
_____
_____

Date:_____/_____/_____

Three things I'm grateful for:

_____
_____
_____
_____

Three things that I did particularly well today:

_____
_____
_____
_____

Three positive things that happened today:

_____
_____
_____
_____

How could I have made today even better?

_____
_____
_____
_____

What is my most important goal for tomorrow?

_____
_____
_____
_____

Date:_____/_____/_____

Three things I'm grateful for:

_____
_____
_____
_____

Three things that I did particularly well today:

_____
_____
_____
_____

Three positive things that happened today:

_____
_____
_____
_____

How could I have made today even better?

_____
_____
_____
_____

What is my most important goal for tomorrow?

_____
_____
_____
_____

Date:_____/_____/_____

Three things I'm grateful for:

_____
_____
_____
_____

Three things that I did particularly well today:

_____
_____
_____
_____

Three positive things that happened today:

_____
_____
_____
_____

How could I have made today even better?

_____
_____
_____
_____

What is my most important goal for tomorrow?

_____
_____
_____
_____

Date:_____/_____/_____

Three things I'm grateful for:

_____
_____
_____
_____

Three things that I did particularly well today:

_____
_____
_____
_____

Three positive things that happened today:

_____
_____
_____
_____

How could I have made today even better?

_____
_____
_____
_____

What is my most important goal for tomorrow?

_____
_____
_____
_____

Week 9

Gratitude is when memory is stored in the heart and not in the mind.

Lionel Hampton

Date:_____/_____/_____

Three things I'm grateful for:

_____
_____
_____
_____

Three things that I did particularly well today:

_____
_____
_____
_____

Three positive things that happened today:

_____
_____
_____
_____

How could I have made today even better?

_____
_____
_____
_____

What is my most important goal for tomorrow?

_____
_____
_____
_____

Date:_____/_____/_____

Three things I'm grateful for:

_____
_____
_____
_____

Three things that I did particularly well today:

_____
_____
_____
_____

Three positive things that happened today:

_____
_____
_____
_____

How could I have made today even better?

_____
_____
_____
_____

What is my most important goal for tomorrow?

_____
_____
_____
_____

Date:_____/_____/_____

Three things I'm grateful for:

_____
_____
_____
_____

Three things that I did particularly well today:

_____
_____
_____
_____

Three positive things that happened today:

_____
_____
_____
_____

How could I have made today even better?

_____
_____
_____
_____

What is my most important goal for tomorrow?

_____
_____
_____
_____

Date:_____/_____/_____

Three things I'm grateful for:

_____
_____
_____
_____

Three things that I did particularly well today:

_____
_____
_____
_____

Three positive things that happened today:

_____
_____
_____
_____

How could I have made today even better?

_____
_____
_____
_____

What is my most important goal for tomorrow?

_____
_____
_____
_____

Date:_____/_____/_____

Three things I'm grateful for:

_____
_____
_____
_____

Three things that I did particularly well today:

_____
_____
_____
_____

Three positive things that happened today:

_____
_____
_____
_____

How could I have made today even better?

_____
_____
_____
_____

What is my most important goal for tomorrow?

_____
_____
_____
_____

Date:_____/_____/_____

Three things I'm grateful for:

_____
_____
_____
_____

Three things that I did particularly well today:

_____
_____
_____
_____

Three positive things that happened today:

_____
_____
_____
_____

How could I have made today even better?

_____
_____
_____
_____

What is my most important goal for tomorrow?

_____
_____
_____
_____

Date:_____/_____/_____

Three things I'm grateful for:

_____
_____
_____
_____

Three things that I did particularly well today:

_____
_____
_____
_____

Three positive things that happened today:

_____
_____
_____
_____

How could I have made today even better?

_____
_____
_____
_____

What is my most important goal for tomorrow?

_____
_____
_____
_____

Week 10

Gratitude is riches. Complaint is poverty.

Doris Day

Date:_____/_____/_____

Three things I'm grateful for:

_____

_____

_____

_____

Three things that I did particularly well today:

_____

_____

_____

_____

Three positive things that happened today:

_____

_____

_____

_____

How could I have made today even better?

_____

_____

_____

_____

What is my most important goal for tomorrow?

_____

_____

_____

_____

Date:_____/_____/_____

Three things I'm grateful for:

_____
_____
_____
_____

Three things that I did particularly well today:

_____
_____
_____
_____

Three positive things that happened today:

_____
_____
_____
_____

How could I have made today even better?

_____
_____
_____
_____

What is my most important goal for tomorrow?

_____
_____
_____
_____

Date:_____/_____/_____

Three things I'm grateful for:

_____
_____
_____
_____

Three things that I did particularly well today:

_____
_____
_____
_____

Three positive things that happened today:

_____
_____
_____
_____

How could I have made today even better?

_____
_____
_____
_____

What is my most important goal for tomorrow?

_____
_____
_____
_____

Date:_____/_____/_____

Three things I'm grateful for:

_____
_____
_____
_____

Three things that I did particularly well today:

_____
_____
_____
_____

Three positive things that happened today:

_____
_____
_____
_____

How could I have made today even better?

_____
_____
_____
_____

What is my most important goal for tomorrow?

_____
_____
_____
_____

Date:_____/_____/_____

Three things I'm grateful for:

_____
_____
_____
_____

Three things that I did particularly well today:

_____
_____
_____
_____

Three positive things that happened today:

_____
_____
_____
_____

How could I have made today even better?

_____
_____
_____
_____

What is my most important goal for tomorrow?

_____
_____
_____
_____

Date:_____/_____/_____

Three things I'm grateful for:

_____

_____

_____

_____

Three things that I did particularly well today:

_____

_____

_____

_____

Three positive things that happened today:

_____

_____

_____

_____

How could I have made today even better?

_____

_____

_____

_____

What is my most important goal for tomorrow?

_____

_____

_____

_____

Date:_____/_____/_____

Three things I'm grateful for:

_____

_____

_____

_____

Three things that I did particularly well today:

_____

_____

_____

_____

Three positive things that happened today:

_____

_____

_____

_____

How could I have made today even better?

_____

_____

_____

_____

What is my most important goal for tomorrow?

_____

_____

_____

_____

Week 11

Be thankful for what you have; you'll end up having more. If you concentrate on what you don't have, you will never, ever have enough.

Oprah Winfrey

Date:_____/_____/_____

Three things I'm grateful for:

_____
_____
_____
_____

Three things that I did particularly well today:

_____
_____
_____
_____

Three positive things that happened today:

_____
_____
_____
_____

How could I have made today even better?

_____
_____
_____
_____

What is my most important goal for tomorrow?

_____
_____
_____
_____

Date:_____/_____/_____

Three things I'm grateful for:

_____

_____

_____

_____

Three things that I did particularly well today:

_____

_____

_____

_____

Three positive things that happened today:

_____

_____

_____

_____

How could I have made today even better?

_____

_____

_____

_____

What is my most important goal for tomorrow?

_____

_____

_____

_____

Date:_____/_____/_____

Three things I'm grateful for:

_____
_____
_____
_____

Three things that I did particularly well today:

_____
_____
_____
_____

Three positive things that happened today:

_____
_____
_____
_____

How could I have made today even better?

_____
_____
_____
_____

What is my most important goal for tomorrow?

_____
_____
_____
_____

Date:_____/_____/_____

Three things I'm grateful for:

_____
_____
_____
_____

Three things that I did particularly well today:

_____
_____
_____
_____

Three positive things that happened today:

_____
_____
_____
_____

How could I have made today even better?

_____
_____
_____
_____

What is my most important goal for tomorrow?

_____
_____
_____
_____

Date:_____/_____/_____

Three things I'm grateful for:

_____
_____
_____
_____

Three things that I did particularly well today:

_____
_____
_____
_____

Three positive things that happened today:

_____
_____
_____
_____

How could I have made today even better?

_____
_____
_____
_____

What is my most important goal for tomorrow?

_____
_____
_____
_____

Date:_____/_____/_____

Three things I'm grateful for:

_____
_____
_____
_____

Three things that I did particularly well today:

_____
_____
_____
_____

Three positive things that happened today:

_____
_____
_____
_____

How could I have made today even better?

_____
_____
_____
_____

What is my most important goal for tomorrow?

_____
_____
_____
_____

Date:_____/_____/_____

Three things I'm grateful for:

_____
_____
_____
_____

Three things that I did particularly well today:

_____
_____
_____
_____

Three positive things that happened today:

_____
_____
_____
_____

How could I have made today even better?

_____
_____
_____
_____

What is my most important goal for tomorrow?

_____
_____
_____
_____

Week 12

Gratitude is not only the greatest of virtues but the parent of all others.

Marcus Tullius Cicero

Date:_____/_____/_____

Three things I'm grateful for:

_____

_____

_____

_____

Three things that I did particularly well today:

_____

_____

_____

_____

Three positive things that happened today:

_____

_____

_____

_____

How could I have made today even better?

_____

_____

_____

_____

What is my most important goal for tomorrow?

_____

_____

_____

_____

Date:_____/_____/_____

Three things I'm grateful for:

_____
_____
_____
_____

Three things that I did particularly well today:

_____
_____
_____
_____

Three positive things that happened today:

_____
_____
_____
_____

How could I have made today even better?

_____
_____
_____
_____

What is my most important goal for tomorrow?

_____
_____
_____
_____

Date:_____/_____/_____

Three things I'm grateful for:

_____

_____

_____

_____

Three things that I did particularly well today:

_____

_____

_____

_____

Three positive things that happened today:

_____

_____

_____

_____

How could I have made today even better?

_____

_____

_____

_____

What is my most important goal for tomorrow?

_____

_____

_____

_____

Date:_____/_____/_____

Three things I'm grateful for:

_____
_____
_____
_____

Three things that I did particularly well today:

_____
_____
_____
_____

Three positive things that happened today:

_____
_____
_____
_____

How could I have made today even better?

_____
_____
_____
_____

What is my most important goal for tomorrow?

_____
_____
_____
_____

Date:_____/_____/_____

Three things I'm grateful for:

_____
_____
_____
_____

Three things that I did particularly well today:

_____
_____
_____
_____

Three positive things that happened today:

_____
_____
_____
_____

How could I have made today even better?

_____
_____
_____
_____

What is my most important goal for tomorrow?

_____
_____
_____
_____

Date:_____/_____/_____

Three things I'm grateful for:

_____

_____

_____

_____

Three things that I did particularly well today:

_____

_____

_____

_____

Three positive things that happened today:

_____

_____

_____

_____

How could I have made today even better?

_____

_____

_____

_____

What is my most important goal for tomorrow?

_____

_____

_____

_____

Date:_____/_____/_____

Three things I'm grateful for:

_____

_____

_____

_____

Three things that I did particularly well today:

_____

_____

_____

_____

Three positive things that happened today:

_____

_____

_____

_____

How could I have made today even better?

_____

_____

_____

_____

What is my most important goal for tomorrow?

_____

_____

_____

_____

Week 13

It is through gratitude for the present moment that the spiritual dimension of life opens up.

Eckhart Tolle

Date:_____/_____/_____

Three things I'm grateful for:

_____
_____
_____
_____

Three things that I did particularly well today:

_____
_____
_____
_____

Three positive things that happened today:

_____
_____
_____
_____

How could I have made today even better?

_____
_____
_____
_____

What is my most important goal for tomorrow?

_____
_____
_____
_____

Date:_____/_____/_____

Three things I'm grateful for:

_____
_____
_____
_____

Three things that I did particularly well today:

_____
_____
_____
_____

Three positive things that happened today:

_____
_____
_____
_____

How could I have made today even better?

_____
_____
_____
_____

What is my most important goal for tomorrow?

_____
_____
_____
_____

Date:_____/_____/_____

Three things I'm grateful for:

_____
_____
_____
_____

Three things that I did particularly well today:

_____
_____
_____
_____

Three positive things that happened today:

_____
_____
_____
_____

How could I have made today even better?

_____
_____
_____
_____

What is my most important goal for tomorrow?

_____
_____
_____
_____

Date:_____/_____/_____

Three things I'm grateful for:

_____
_____
_____
_____

Three things that I did particularly well today:

_____
_____
_____
_____

Three positive things that happened today:

_____
_____
_____
_____

How could I have made today even better?

_____
_____
_____
_____

What is my most important goal for tomorrow?

_____
_____
_____
_____

Date:_____/_____/_____

Three things I'm grateful for:

_____
_____
_____
_____

Three things that I did particularly well today:

_____
_____
_____
_____

Three positive things that happened today:

_____
_____
_____
_____

How could I have made today even better?

_____
_____
_____
_____

What is my most important goal for tomorrow?

_____
_____
_____
_____

Date:_____/_____/_____

Three things I'm grateful for:

_____
_____
_____
_____

Three things that I did particularly well today:

_____
_____
_____
_____

Three positive things that happened today:

_____
_____
_____
_____

How could I have made today even better?

_____
_____
_____
_____

What is my most important goal for tomorrow?

_____
_____
_____
_____

Date:_____/_____/_____

Three things I'm grateful for:

_____
_____
_____
_____

Three things that I did particularly well today:

_____
_____
_____
_____

Three positive things that happened today:

_____
_____
_____
_____

How could I have made today even better?

_____
_____
_____
_____

What is my most important goal for tomorrow?

_____
_____
_____
_____

Week 14

Gratitude helps you to grow and expand; gratitude brings joy and laughter into your life and into the lives of all those around you.

Eileen Caddy

Date:_____/_____/_____

Three things I'm grateful for:

_____
_____
_____
_____

Three things that I did particularly well today:

_____
_____
_____
_____

Three positive things that happened today:

_____
_____
_____
_____

How could I have made today even better?

_____
_____
_____
_____

What is my most important goal for tomorrow?

_____
_____
_____
_____

Date:_____/_____/_____

Three things I'm grateful for:

_____
_____
_____
_____

Three things that I did particularly well today:

_____
_____
_____
_____

Three positive things that happened today:

_____
_____
_____
_____

How could I have made today even better?

_____
_____
_____
_____

What is my most important goal for tomorrow?

_____
_____
_____
_____

Date:_____/_____/_____

Three things I'm grateful for:

_____
_____
_____
_____

Three things that I did particularly well today:

_____
_____
_____
_____

Three positive things that happened today:

_____
_____
_____
_____

How could I have made today even better?

_____
_____
_____
_____

What is my most important goal for tomorrow?

_____
_____
_____
_____

Date:_____/_____/_____

Three things I'm grateful for:

_____
_____
_____
_____

Three things that I did particularly well today:

_____
_____
_____
_____

Three positive things that happened today:

_____
_____
_____
_____

How could I have made today even better?

_____
_____
_____
_____

What is my most important goal for tomorrow?

_____
_____
_____
_____

Date:_____/_____/_____

Three things I'm grateful for:

_____
_____
_____
_____

Three things that I did particularly well today:

_____
_____
_____
_____

Three positive things that happened today:

_____
_____
_____
_____

How could I have made today even better?

_____
_____
_____
_____

What is my most important goal for tomorrow?

_____
_____
_____
_____

Date:_____/_____/_____

Three things I'm grateful for:

_____
_____
_____
_____

Three things that I did particularly well today:

_____
_____
_____
_____

Three positive things that happened today:

_____
_____
_____
_____

How could I have made today even better?

_____
_____
_____
_____

What is my most important goal for tomorrow?

_____
_____
_____
_____

Date:_____/_____/_____

Three things I'm grateful for:

_____
_____
_____
_____

Three things that I did particularly well today:

_____
_____
_____
_____

Three positive things that happened today:

_____
_____
_____
_____

How could I have made today even better?

_____
_____
_____
_____

What is my most important goal for tomorrow?

_____
_____
_____
_____

Week 15

Often people ask how I manage to be happy despite having no arms and no legs. The quick answer is that I have a choice. I can be angry about not having limbs, or I can be thankful that I have a purpose. I chose gratitude.

Nick Vujicic

Date:_____/_____/_____

Three things I'm grateful for:

_____

_____

_____

_____

Three things that I did particularly well today:

_____

_____

_____

_____

Three positive things that happened today:

_____

_____

_____

_____

How could I have made today even better?

_____

_____

_____

_____

What is my most important goal for tomorrow?

_____

_____

_____

_____

Date:_____/_____/_____

Three things I'm grateful for:

_____
_____
_____
_____

Three things that I did particularly well today:

_____
_____
_____
_____

Three positive things that happened today:

_____
_____
_____
_____

How could I have made today even better?

_____
_____
_____
_____

What is my most important goal for tomorrow?

_____
_____
_____
_____

Date:_____/_____/_____

Three things I'm grateful for:

_____

_____

_____

_____

Three things that I did particularly well today:

_____

_____

_____

_____

Three positive things that happened today:

_____

_____

_____

_____

How could I have made today even better?

_____

_____

_____

_____

What is my most important goal for tomorrow?

_____

_____

_____

_____

Date:_____ /_____ /_____

Three things I'm grateful for:
_____
_____
_____
_____

Three things that I did particularly well today:
_____
_____
_____
_____

Three positive things that happened today:
_____
_____
_____
_____

How could I have made today even better?
_____
_____
_____
_____

What is my most important goal for tomorrow?
_____
_____
_____
_____

Date:_____/_____/_____

Three things I'm grateful for:

_____
_____
_____
_____

Three things that I did particularly well today:

_____
_____
_____
_____

Three positive things that happened today:

_____
_____
_____
_____

How could I have made today even better?

_____
_____
_____
_____

What is my most important goal for tomorrow?

_____
_____
_____
_____

Date:_____/_____/_____

Three things I'm grateful for:

_____
_____
_____
_____

Three things that I did particularly well today:

_____
_____
_____
_____

Three positive things that happened today:

_____
_____
_____
_____

How could I have made today even better?

_____
_____
_____
_____

What is my most important goal for tomorrow?

_____
_____
_____
_____

Date:_____/_____/_____

Three things I'm grateful for:

_____

_____

_____

_____

Three things that I did particularly well today:

_____

_____

_____

_____

Three positive things that happened today:

_____

_____

_____

_____

How could I have made today even better?

_____

_____

_____

_____

What is my most important goal for tomorrow?

_____

_____

_____

_____

Week 16

The discipline of gratitude is the explicit effort to acknowledge that all I am and have is given to me as a gift of love, a gift to be celebrated with joy.

Henri Nouwen

Date:_____/_____/_____

Three things I'm grateful for:

_____

_____

_____

_____

Three things that I did particularly well today:

_____

_____

_____

_____

Three positive things that happened today:

_____

_____

_____

_____

How could I have made today even better?

_____

_____

_____

_____

What is my most important goal for tomorrow?

_____

_____

_____

_____

Date:_____/_____/_____

Three things I'm grateful for:

_____
_____
_____
_____

Three things that I did particularly well today:

_____
_____
_____
_____

Three positive things that happened today:

_____
_____
_____
_____

How could I have made today even better?

_____
_____
_____
_____

What is my most important goal for tomorrow?

_____
_____
_____
_____

Date:_____/_____/_____

Three things I'm grateful for:

_____

_____

_____

_____

Three things that I did particularly well today:

_____

_____

_____

_____

Three positive things that happened today:

_____

_____

_____

_____

How could I have made today even better?

_____

_____

_____

_____

What is my most important goal for tomorrow?

_____

_____

_____

_____

Date:_____/_____/_____

Three things I'm grateful for:

_____
_____
_____
_____

Three things that I did particularly well today:

_____
_____
_____
_____

Three positive things that happened today:

_____
_____
_____
_____

How could I have made today even better?

_____
_____
_____
_____

What is my most important goal for tomorrow?

_____
_____
_____
_____

Date:_____/_____/_____

Three things I'm grateful for:

_____
_____
_____
_____

Three things that I did particularly well today:

_____
_____
_____
_____

Three positive things that happened today:

_____
_____
_____
_____

How could I have made today even better?

_____
_____
_____
_____

What is my most important goal for tomorrow?

_____
_____
_____
_____

Date:_____/_____/_____

Three things I'm grateful for:

_____

_____

_____

_____

Three things that I did particularly well today:

_____

_____

_____

_____

Three positive things that happened today:

_____

_____

_____

_____

How could I have made today even better?

_____

_____

_____

_____

What is my most important goal for tomorrow?

_____

_____

_____

_____

Date:_____/_____/_____

Three things I'm grateful for:

_____
_____
_____
_____

Three things that I did particularly well today:

_____
_____
_____
_____

Three positive things that happened today:

_____
_____
_____
_____

How could I have made today even better?

_____
_____
_____
_____

What is my most important goal for tomorrow?

_____
_____
_____
_____

Week 17

Gratitude is the healthiest of all human emotions.
The more you express gratitude for what you have,
the more likely you will have even more to express
gratitude for.

Zig Ziglar

Date:_____/_____/_____

Three things I'm grateful for:

_____
_____
_____
_____

Three things that I did particularly well today:

_____
_____
_____
_____

Three positive things that happened today:

_____
_____
_____
_____

How could I have made today even better?

_____
_____
_____
_____

What is my most important goal for tomorrow?

_____
_____
_____
_____

Date:_____/_____/_____

Three things I'm grateful for:

_____
_____
_____
_____

Three things that I did particularly well today:

_____
_____
_____
_____

Three positive things that happened today:

_____
_____
_____
_____

How could I have made today even better?

_____
_____
_____
_____

What is my most important goal for tomorrow?

_____
_____
_____
_____

Date:_____/_____/_____

Three things I'm grateful for:

_____

_____

_____

_____

Three things that I did particularly well today:

_____

_____

_____

_____

Three positive things that happened today:

_____

_____

_____

_____

How could I have made today even better?

_____

_____

_____

_____

What is my most important goal for tomorrow?

_____

_____

_____

_____

Date:_____/_____/_____

Three things I'm grateful for:

_____
_____
_____
_____

Three things that I did particularly well today:

_____
_____
_____
_____

Three positive things that happened today:

_____
_____
_____
_____

How could I have made today even better?

_____
_____
_____
_____

What is my most important goal for tomorrow?

_____
_____
_____
_____

Date:_____/_____/_____

Three things I'm grateful for:

_____
_____
_____
_____

Three things that I did particularly well today:

_____
_____
_____
_____

Three positive things that happened today:

_____
_____
_____
_____

How could I have made today even better?

_____
_____
_____
_____

What is my most important goal for tomorrow?

_____
_____
_____
_____

Date:_____/_____/_____

Three things I'm grateful for:

_____
_____
_____
_____

Three things that I did particularly well today:

_____
_____
_____
_____

Three positive things that happened today:

_____
_____
_____
_____

How could I have made today even better?

_____
_____
_____
_____

What is my most important goal for tomorrow?

_____
_____
_____
_____

Date:_____/_____/_____

Three things I'm grateful for:

_____
_____
_____
_____

Three things that I did particularly well today:

_____
_____
_____
_____

Three positive things that happened today:

_____
_____
_____
_____

How could I have made today even better?

_____
_____
_____
_____

What is my most important goal for tomorrow?

_____
_____
_____
_____

Week 18

Gratitude practice is really, really important to me. I think it's an incredible way to start your day.

Rachel Hollis

Date:_____/_____/_____

Three things I'm grateful for:

_____
_____
_____
_____

Three things that I did particularly well today:

_____
_____
_____
_____

Three positive things that happened today:

_____
_____
_____
_____

How could I have made today even better?

_____
_____
_____
_____

What is my most important goal for tomorrow?

_____
_____
_____
_____

Date:_____/_____/_____

Three things I'm grateful for:

_____

_____

_____

_____

Three things that I did particularly well today:

_____

_____

_____

_____

Three positive things that happened today:

_____

_____

_____

_____

How could I have made today even better?

_____

_____

_____

_____

What is my most important goal for tomorrow?

_____

_____

_____

_____

Date:_____/_____/_____

Three things I'm grateful for:

_____
_____
_____
_____

Three things that I did particularly well today:

_____
_____
_____
_____

Three positive things that happened today:

_____
_____
_____
_____

How could I have made today even better?

_____
_____
_____
_____

What is my most important goal for tomorrow?

_____
_____
_____
_____

Date:_____/_____/_____

Three things I'm grateful for:

_____
_____
_____
_____

Three things that I did particularly well today:

_____
_____
_____
_____

Three positive things that happened today:

_____
_____
_____
_____

How could I have made today even better?

_____
_____
_____
_____

What is my most important goal for tomorrow?

_____
_____
_____
_____

Date:_____/_____/_____

Three things I'm grateful for:

_____
_____
_____
_____

Three things that I did particularly well today:

_____
_____
_____
_____

Three positive things that happened today:

_____
_____
_____
_____

How could I have made today even better?

_____
_____
_____
_____

What is my most important goal for tomorrow?

_____
_____
_____
_____

Date:_____ / _____ / _____

Three things I'm grateful for:

_____
_____
_____
_____

Three things that I did particularly well today:

_____
_____
_____
_____

Three positive things that happened today:

_____
_____
_____
_____

How could I have made today even better?

_____
_____
_____
_____

What is my most important goal for tomorrow?

_____
_____
_____
_____

Date:_____/_____/_____

Three things I'm grateful for:

_____

_____

_____

_____

Three things that I did particularly well today:

_____

_____

_____

_____

Three positive things that happened today:

_____

_____

_____

_____

How could I have made today even better?

_____

_____

_____

_____

What is my most important goal for tomorrow?

_____

_____

_____

_____

Week 19

A smart manager will establish a culture of gratitude. Expand the appreciative attitude to suppliers, vendors, delivery people, and of course, customers.

Harvey Mackay

Date:_____/_____/_____

Three things I'm grateful for:

_____

_____

_____

_____

Three things that I did particularly well today:

_____

_____

_____

_____

Three positive things that happened today:

_____

_____

_____

_____

How could I have made today even better?

_____

_____

_____

_____

What is my most important goal for tomorrow?

_____

_____

_____

_____

Date:_____/_____/_____

Three things I'm grateful for:

_____
_____
_____
_____

Three things that I did particularly well today:

_____
_____
_____
_____

Three positive things that happened today:

_____
_____
_____
_____

How could I have made today even better?

_____
_____
_____
_____

What is my most important goal for tomorrow?

_____
_____
_____
_____

Date:_____/_____/_____

Three things I'm grateful for:

_____
_____
_____
_____

Three things that I did particularly well today:

_____
_____
_____
_____

Three positive things that happened today:

_____
_____
_____
_____

How could I have made today even better?

_____
_____
_____
_____

What is my most important goal for tomorrow?

_____
_____
_____
_____

Date:_____ / _____ / _____

Three things I'm grateful for:

_____

_____

_____

_____

Three things that I did particularly well today:

_____

_____

_____

_____

Three positive things that happened today:

_____

_____

_____

_____

How could I have made today even better?

_____

_____

_____

_____

What is my most important goal for tomorrow?

_____

_____

_____

_____

Date:_____/_____/_____

Three things I'm grateful for:

_____
_____
_____
_____

Three things that I did particularly well today:

_____
_____
_____
_____

Three positive things that happened today:

_____
_____
_____
_____

How could I have made today even better?

_____
_____
_____
_____

What is my most important goal for tomorrow?

_____
_____
_____
_____

Date:_____/_____/_____

Three things I'm grateful for:

_____
_____
_____
_____

Three things that I did particularly well today:

_____
_____
_____
_____

Three positive things that happened today:

_____
_____
_____
_____

How could I have made today even better?

_____
_____
_____
_____

What is my most important goal for tomorrow?

_____
_____
_____
_____

Date:_____/_____/_____

Three things I'm grateful for:

_____

_____

_____

_____

Three things that I did particularly well today:

_____

_____

_____

_____

Three positive things that happened today:

_____

_____

_____

_____

How could I have made today even better?

_____

_____

_____

_____

What is my most important goal for tomorrow?

_____

_____

_____

_____

Week 20

At the age of 18, I made up my mind to never have another bad day in my life. I dove into an endless sea of gratitude from which I've never emerged.

Patch Adams

Date:_____/_____/_____

Three things I'm grateful for:

_____
_____
_____
_____

Three things that I did particularly well today:

_____
_____
_____
_____

Three positive things that happened today:

_____
_____
_____
_____

How could I have made today even better?

_____
_____
_____
_____

What is my most important goal for tomorrow?

_____
_____
_____
_____

Date:_____/_____/_____

Three things I'm grateful for:

_____
_____
_____
_____

Three things that I did particularly well today:

_____
_____
_____
_____

Three positive things that happened today:

_____
_____
_____
_____

How could I have made today even better?

_____
_____
_____
_____

What is my most important goal for tomorrow?

_____
_____
_____
_____

Date:_____/_____/_____

Three things I'm grateful for:

_____
_____
_____
_____

Three things that I did particularly well today:

_____
_____
_____
_____

Three positive things that happened today:

_____
_____
_____
_____

How could I have made today even better?

_____
_____
_____
_____

What is my most important goal for tomorrow?

_____
_____
_____
_____

Date:_____/_____/_____

Three things I'm grateful for:

_____
_____
_____
_____

Three things that I did particularly well today:

_____
_____
_____
_____

Three positive things that happened today:

_____
_____
_____
_____

How could I have made today even better?

_____
_____
_____
_____

What is my most important goal for tomorrow?

_____
_____
_____
_____

Date:_____/_____/_____

Three things I'm grateful for:

_____
_____
_____
_____

Three things that I did particularly well today:

_____
_____
_____
_____

Three positive things that happened today:

_____
_____
_____
_____

How could I have made today even better?

_____
_____
_____
_____

What is my most important goal for tomorrow?

_____
_____
_____
_____

Date:_____/_____/_____

Three things I'm grateful for:

_____
_____
_____
_____

Three things that I did particularly well today:

_____
_____
_____
_____

Three positive things that happened today:

_____
_____
_____
_____

How could I have made today even better?

_____
_____
_____
_____

What is my most important goal for tomorrow?

_____
_____
_____
_____

Date:_____/_____/_____

Three things I'm grateful for:

_____
_____
_____
_____

Three things that I did particularly well today:

_____
_____
_____
_____

Three positive things that happened today:

_____
_____
_____
_____

How could I have made today even better?

_____
_____
_____
_____

What is my most important goal for tomorrow?

_____
_____
_____
_____

Week 21

When it comes to life the critical thing is whether you take things for granted or take them with gratitude.

Gilbert K. Chesterton

Date:_____/_____/_____

Three things I'm grateful for:

_____
_____
_____
_____

Three things that I did particularly well today:

_____
_____
_____
_____

Three positive things that happened today:

_____
_____
_____
_____

How could I have made today even better?

_____
_____
_____
_____

What is my most important goal for tomorrow?

_____
_____
_____
_____

Date:_____/_____/_____

Three things I'm grateful for:

_____
_____
_____
_____

Three things that I did particularly well today:

_____
_____
_____
_____

Three positive things that happened today:

_____
_____
_____
_____

How could I have made today even better?

_____
_____
_____
_____

What is my most important goal for tomorrow?

_____
_____
_____
_____

Date:_____/_____/_____

Three things I'm grateful for:

_____
_____
_____
_____

Three things that I did particularly well today:

_____
_____
_____
_____

Three positive things that happened today:

_____
_____
_____
_____

How could I have made today even better?

_____
_____
_____
_____

What is my most important goal for tomorrow?

_____
_____
_____
_____

Date:_____/_____/_____

Three things I'm grateful for:

_____
_____
_____
_____

Three things that I did particularly well today:

_____
_____
_____
_____

Three positive things that happened today:

_____
_____
_____
_____

How could I have made today even better?

_____
_____
_____
_____

What is my most important goal for tomorrow?

_____
_____
_____
_____

Date:_____/_____/_____

Three things I'm grateful for:

_____
_____
_____
_____

Three things that I did particularly well today:

_____
_____
_____
_____

Three positive things that happened today:

_____
_____
_____
_____

How could I have made today even better?

_____
_____
_____
_____

What is my most important goal for tomorrow?

_____
_____
_____
_____

Date:_____/_____/_____

Three things I'm grateful for:

_____
_____
_____
_____

Three things that I did particularly well today:

_____
_____
_____
_____

Three positive things that happened today:

_____
_____
_____
_____

How could I have made today even better?

_____
_____
_____
_____

What is my most important goal for tomorrow?

_____
_____
_____
_____

Date:_____/_____/_____

Three things I'm grateful for:

_____
_____
_____
_____

Three things that I did particularly well today:

_____
_____
_____
_____

Three positive things that happened today:

_____
_____
_____
_____

How could I have made today even better?

_____
_____
_____
_____

What is my most important goal for tomorrow?

_____
_____
_____
_____

Week 22

I'm in a constant state of gratitude.

Mandy Patinkin

Date:_____/_____/_____

Three things I'm grateful for:

_____
_____
_____
_____

Three things that I did particularly well today:

_____
_____
_____
_____

Three positive things that happened today:

_____
_____
_____
_____

How could I have made today even better?

_____
_____
_____
_____

What is my most important goal for tomorrow?

_____
_____
_____
_____

Date:_____/_____/_____

Three things I'm grateful for:

_____

_____

_____

_____

Three things that I did particularly well today:

_____

_____

_____

_____

Three positive things that happened today:

_____

_____

_____

_____

How could I have made today even better?

_____

_____

_____

_____

What is my most important goal for tomorrow?

_____

_____

_____

_____

Date:_____/_____/_____

Three things I'm grateful for:

_____

_____

_____

_____

Three things that I did particularly well today:

_____

_____

_____

_____

Three positive things that happened today:

_____

_____

_____

_____

How could I have made today even better?

_____

_____

_____

_____

What is my most important goal for tomorrow?

_____

_____

_____

_____

Date:_____/_____/_____

Three things I'm grateful for:

_____
_____
_____
_____

Three things that I did particularly well today:

_____
_____
_____
_____

Three positive things that happened today:

_____
_____
_____
_____

How could I have made today even better?

_____
_____
_____
_____

What is my most important goal for tomorrow?

_____
_____
_____
_____

Date:_____/_____/_____

Three things I'm grateful for:

_____

_____

_____

_____

Three things that I did particularly well today:

_____

_____

_____

_____

Three positive things that happened today:

_____

_____

_____

_____

How could I have made today even better?

_____

_____

_____

_____

What is my most important goal for tomorrow?

_____

_____

_____

_____

Date:_____/_____/_____

Three things I'm grateful for:

_____
_____
_____
_____

Three things that I did particularly well today:

_____
_____
_____
_____

Three positive things that happened today:

_____
_____
_____
_____

How could I have made today even better?

_____
_____
_____
_____

What is my most important goal for tomorrow?

_____
_____
_____
_____

Date:_____/_____/_____

Three things I'm grateful for:

_____

_____

_____

_____

Three things that I did particularly well today:

_____

_____

_____

_____

Three positive things that happened today:

_____

_____

_____

_____

How could I have made today even better?

_____

_____

_____

_____

What is my most important goal for tomorrow?

_____

_____

_____

_____

Week 23

When we focus on our gratitude, the tide of disappointment goes out and the tide of love rushes in.

Kristin Armstrong

Date:_____/_____/_____

Three things I'm grateful for:

_____
_____
_____
_____

Three things that I did particularly well today:

_____
_____
_____
_____

Three positive things that happened today:

_____
_____
_____
_____

How could I have made today even better?

_____
_____
_____
_____

What is my most important goal for tomorrow?

_____
_____
_____
_____

Date:_____/_____/_____

Three things I'm grateful for:

_____
_____
_____
_____

Three things that I did particularly well today:

_____
_____
_____
_____

Three positive things that happened today:

_____
_____
_____
_____

How could I have made today even better?

_____
_____
_____
_____

What is my most important goal for tomorrow?

_____
_____
_____
_____

Date:_____/_____/_____

Three things I'm grateful for:

_____
_____
_____
_____

Three things that I did particularly well today:

_____
_____
_____
_____

Three positive things that happened today:

_____
_____
_____
_____

How could I have made today even better?

_____
_____
_____
_____

What is my most important goal for tomorrow?

_____
_____
_____
_____

Date:_____/_____/_____

Three things I'm grateful for:

_____

_____

_____

_____

Three things that I did particularly well today:

_____

_____

_____

_____

Three positive things that happened today:

_____

_____

_____

_____

How could I have made today even better?

_____

_____

_____

_____

What is my most important goal for tomorrow?

_____

_____

_____

_____

Date:_____/_____/_____

Three things I'm grateful for:

_____

_____

_____

_____

Three things that I did particularly well today:

_____

_____

_____

_____

Three positive things that happened today:

_____

_____

_____

_____

How could I have made today even better?

_____

_____

_____

_____

What is my most important goal for tomorrow?

_____

_____

_____

_____

Date:_____/_____/_____

Three things I'm grateful for:

_____
_____
_____
_____

Three things that I did particularly well today:

_____
_____
_____
_____

Three positive things that happened today:

_____
_____
_____
_____

How could I have made today even better?

_____
_____
_____
_____

What is my most important goal for tomorrow?

_____
_____
_____
_____

Date:_____/_____/_____

Three things I'm grateful for:

_____
_____
_____
_____

Three things that I did particularly well today:

_____
_____
_____
_____

Three positive things that happened today:

_____
_____
_____
_____

How could I have made today even better?

_____
_____
_____
_____

What is my most important goal for tomorrow?

_____
_____
_____
_____

Week 24

No one ever said learning was to be easy, but it's part of the process of evolving as a human being, and we all have to go through it. When I look back, I see that each difficult time brought an important lesson. And I prefer to look at it with gratitude because I wouldn't be who I am today if I haven't gone through it all.

Gisele Bundchen

Date:_____/_____/_____

Three things I'm grateful for:

_____

_____

_____

_____

Three things that I did particularly well today:

_____

_____

_____

_____

Three positive things that happened today:

_____

_____

_____

_____

How could I have made today even better?

_____

_____

_____

_____

What is my most important goal for tomorrow?

_____

_____

_____

_____

Date:_____/_____/_____

Three things I'm grateful for:

_____

_____

_____

_____

Three things that I did particularly well today:

_____

_____

_____

_____

Three positive things that happened today:

_____

_____

_____

_____

How could I have made today even better?

_____

_____

_____

_____

What is my most important goal for tomorrow?

_____

_____

_____

_____

Date:_____/_____/_____

Three things I'm grateful for:

_____
_____
_____
_____

Three things that I did particularly well today:

_____
_____
_____
_____

Three positive things that happened today:

_____
_____
_____
_____

How could I have made today even better?

_____
_____
_____
_____

What is my most important goal for tomorrow?

_____
_____
_____
_____

Date:_____/_____/_____

Three things I'm grateful for:

_____

_____

_____

_____

Three things that I did particularly well today:

_____

_____

_____

_____

Three positive things that happened today:

_____

_____

_____

_____

How could I have made today even better?

_____

_____

_____

_____

What is my most important goal for tomorrow?

_____

_____

_____

_____

Date:_____/_____/_____

Three things I'm grateful for:

_____
_____
_____
_____

Three things that I did particularly well today:

_____
_____
_____
_____

Three positive things that happened today:

_____
_____
_____
_____

How could I have made today even better?

_____
_____
_____
_____

What is my most important goal for tomorrow?

_____
_____
_____
_____

Date:_____/_____/_____

Three things I'm grateful for:

_____
_____
_____
_____

Three things that I did particularly well today:

_____
_____
_____
_____

Three positive things that happened today:

_____
_____
_____
_____

How could I have made today even better?

_____
_____
_____
_____

What is my most important goal for tomorrow?

_____
_____
_____
_____

Date:_____/_____/_____

Three things I'm grateful for:

_____
_____
_____
_____

Three things that I did particularly well today:

_____
_____
_____
_____

Three positive things that happened today:

_____
_____
_____
_____

How could I have made today even better?

_____
_____
_____
_____

What is my most important goal for tomorrow?

_____
_____
_____
_____

Week 25

I may not be the number one movie star, or my films might not be doing too good. I am grateful for what life has offered me. I have got a great family, parents are together, have a great sister, I get to holiday. All these things make me grateful towards life, for everything. I always say - have an attitude of gratitude.

Sonam Kapoor

Date:_____/_____/_____

Three things I'm grateful for:

_____
_____
_____
_____

Three things that I did particularly well today:

_____
_____
_____
_____

Three positive things that happened today:

_____
_____
_____
_____

How could I have made today even better?

_____
_____
_____
_____

What is my most important goal for tomorrow?

_____
_____
_____
_____

Date:_____/_____/_____

Three things I'm grateful for:

_____

_____

_____

_____

Three things that I did particularly well today:

_____

_____

_____

_____

Three positive things that happened today:

_____

_____

_____

_____

How could I have made today even better?

_____

_____

_____

_____

What is my most important goal for tomorrow?

_____

_____

_____

_____

Date:_____ / _____ / _____

Three things I'm grateful for:

_____

_____

_____

_____

Three things that I did particularly well today:

_____

_____

_____

_____

Three positive things that happened today:

_____

_____

_____

_____

How could I have made today even better?

_____

_____

_____

_____

What is my most important goal for tomorrow?

_____

_____

_____

_____

Date:_____/_____/_____

Three things I'm grateful for:

_____
_____
_____
_____

Three things that I did particularly well today:

_____
_____
_____
_____

Three positive things that happened today:

_____
_____
_____
_____

How could I have made today even better?

_____
_____
_____
_____

What is my most important goal for tomorrow?

_____
_____
_____
_____

Date:_____/_____/_____

Three things I'm grateful for:

_____
_____
_____
_____

Three things that I did particularly well today:

_____
_____
_____
_____

Three positive things that happened today:

_____
_____
_____
_____

How could I have made today even better?

_____
_____
_____
_____

What is my most important goal for tomorrow?

_____
_____
_____
_____

Date:_____/_____/_____

Three things I'm grateful for:

_____

_____

_____

_____

Three things that I did particularly well today:

_____

_____

_____

_____

Three positive things that happened today:

_____

_____

_____

_____

How could I have made today even better?

_____

_____

_____

_____

What is my most important goal for tomorrow?

_____

_____

_____

_____

Date:_____/_____/_____

Three things I'm grateful for:

_____
_____
_____
_____

Three things that I did particularly well today:

_____
_____
_____
_____

Three positive things that happened today:

_____
_____
_____
_____

How could I have made today even better?

_____
_____
_____
_____

What is my most important goal for tomorrow?

_____
_____
_____
_____

Week 26

Let us rise up and be thankful, for if we didn't learn a lot today, at least we learned a little, and if we didn't learn a little, at least we didn't get sick, and if we got sick, at least we didn't die; so, let us all be thankful.

Buddha

Date:_____/_____/_____

Three things I'm grateful for:

_____
_____
_____
_____

Three things that I did particularly well today:

_____
_____
_____
_____

Three positive things that happened today:

_____
_____
_____
_____

How could I have made today even better?

_____
_____
_____
_____

What is my most important goal for tomorrow?

_____
_____
_____
_____

Date:_____/_____/_____

Three things I'm grateful for:

_____
_____
_____
_____

Three things that I did particularly well today:

_____
_____
_____
_____

Three positive things that happened today:

_____
_____
_____
_____

How could I have made today even better?

_____
_____
_____
_____

What is my most important goal for tomorrow?

_____
_____
_____
_____

Date:_____/_____/_____

Three things I'm grateful for:

_____
_____
_____
_____

Three things that I did particularly well today:

_____
_____
_____
_____

Three positive things that happened today:

_____
_____
_____
_____

How could I have made today even better?

_____
_____
_____
_____

What is my most important goal for tomorrow?

_____
_____
_____
_____

Date:_____/_____/_____

Three things I'm grateful for:

_____
_____
_____
_____

Three things that I did particularly well today:

_____
_____
_____
_____

Three positive things that happened today:

_____
_____
_____
_____

How could I have made today even better?

_____
_____
_____
_____

What is my most important goal for tomorrow?

_____
_____
_____
_____

Date:_____/_____/_____

Three things I'm grateful for:

_____
_____
_____
_____

Three things that I did particularly well today:

_____
_____
_____
_____

Three positive things that happened today:

_____
_____
_____
_____

How could I have made today even better?

_____
_____
_____
_____

What is my most important goal for tomorrow?

_____
_____
_____
_____

Date:_____/_____/_____

Three things I'm grateful for:

_____

_____

_____

_____

Three things that I did particularly well today:

_____

_____

_____

_____

Three positive things that happened today:

_____

_____

_____

_____

How could I have made today even better?

_____

_____

_____

_____

What is my most important goal for tomorrow?

_____

_____

_____

_____

Date:_____/_____/_____

Three things I'm grateful for:

_____

_____

_____

_____

Three things that I did particularly well today:

_____

_____

_____

_____

Three positive things that happened today:

_____

_____

_____

_____

How could I have made today even better?

_____

_____

_____

_____

What is my most important goal for tomorrow?

_____

_____

_____

_____

One last thing...

If you have been inspired by this book and want to help others to reach their goals and improve their lives, here are some action steps you can take immediately to make a positive difference:

- Gift it to friends, family, colleagues and even strangers so that they can also learn that they con reach their goals and live great lives.

- Please share your thoughts about this book on Twitter, Facebook and Instagram or write a book review. It helps other people to find it.

- If you own a business or if you are a manager - or even if you're not - gift some copies to your team or employees and improve the productivity of your company.
  Contact me at marc@marcreklau.com. I'll give you a 30% discount on bulk orders.

- If you have a Podcast or know somebody that has one ask them to interview me. I'm always happy to spread the message of 30 DAYS and help people improve their lives. You can also ask you local newspaper, radio station, or online media outlets to interview me :)

About the Author

Marc Reklau is a Coach, Speaker, and author of 9 books including the international #1 Bestseller *"30 Days - Change your habits, change your life"*, which since April 2015 has been sold and downloaded over 200,000 times and has been translated into Spanish, German, Japanese, Chinese, Russian, Thai, Indonesian, Portuguese and Korean among others.

He wrote the book in 2014 after being fired from his job and literally went from jobless to Bestseller (which is actually the title of his second book).

The Spanish version of his book "Destination Happiness" has been published by Spain's #1 Publisher Planeta in January 2018.

Marc's mission is to empower people to create the life they want and to give them the resources and tools to make it happen.

His message is simple: Many people want to change things in their lives, but few are willing to do a simple set of exercises constantly over a period of time. You can plan and create success and happiness in your life by installing habits that support you on the way to your goals.

You can connect with him on Twitter @MarcReklau, Facebook, Instagram or on his website www.goodhabitsacademy.com

You may also like:

30 Days - Change your habits, change your life
Contains the best strategies to help you to create the life you want. The book is based on science, neuroscience, positive psychology and real-life examples and contains the best exercises to quickly create momentum towards a happier, healthier and wealthier life. Thirty days can really make a difference if you do things consistently and develop new habits!

More than 200,000 combined sales and downloads since March 2015.

From Jobless to Amazon Bestseller
From Jobless to Amazon Bestseller shows you the simple, step-by-step system that author Marc Reklau used to write, self publish, market and promote his books to over 200,000 combined sales and downloads on Amazon.

The Productivity Revolution
What if you could dramatically increase your productivity? What if you could stop being overwhelmed and get an extra hour a day to do the things you love? What would finally having time to spend with your family, some alone time to read, or exercise mean to you? Learn the best strategies to double your productivity and get things done in this book.

More than 10,000 copies sold!

Destination Happiness
In Destination Happiness bestselling author, Marc Reklau, shows you scientifically proven exercises and habits that help you to achieve a successful, meaningful and happy life. Science has proven that Happiness and Optimism can be learned. Learn the best and scientifically proven methods to improve your life now and don't be fooled by the simplicity of some of the exercises!

Love Yourself First!

Having healthy self-esteem is being happy with ourselves and believing that we deserve to enjoy the good things in life, exactly like every other person on this planet. Our self-esteem impacts every area of our life: our self-confidence, our relationships with other, the partner or job we choose, our happiness, our inner peace and even our personal and professional success. This book shows you in a very simple and fun way how to raise your self-esteem by doing some of the little exercises it presents to you.

How to become a people Magnet

"How to become a People Magnet" reveals the secrets and psychology behind successful relationships with other people. Your success and happiness in life - at home and in business -, to a great extent, depend on how you get along with other people. **The most successful people**, quite often, aren't the ones with superior intelligence or the best skills, and the happiest people most times aren't smarter than we are, yet they **are the ones who have the greatest people skills.**

Sold over 1300 copies in the month of its launch.

The Life-changing Power of Gratitude

"The Life-Changing Power of Gratitude" **reveals the scientifically proven benefits of gratitude.** Gratitude is considered **the single best - and most impactful - intervention** of the science of positive psychology. Being grateful for everything you have in life and even the things you don't have yet will change everything. **The more grateful you become, the better your life will get.**
You will learn seven simple exercises that will help you to reap the scientifically-proven benefits of gratitude like being happier, sleeping better, getting rid of headaches and anxiety, and much more.

Made in the USA
Columbia, SC
01 November 2019